JUNE 2013

# NATIONAL INSTITUTE OF JUSTICE
# RESEARCH
## IN BRIEF

# Understanding Elder Abuse

## NEW DIRECTIONS FOR DEVELOPING THEORIES OF ELDER ABUSE OCCURRING IN DOMESTIC SETTINGS

BY SHELLY L. JACKSON, PH.D., AND THOMAS L. HAFEMEISTER, J.D., PH.D.

Findings and conclusions of the research reported here are those of the authors and do not necessarily reflect the official position or policies of the U.S. Department of Justice. This research was supported by NIJ under grant number 2006-WG-BX-0010.

NCJ 241731

# Understanding
# Elder Abuse

## NEW DIRECTIONS FOR DEVELOPING THEORIES OF
## ELDER ABUSE OCCURRING IN DOMESTIC SETTINGS

BY SHELLY L. JACKSON, PH.D., AND THOMAS L. HAFEMEISTER, J.D., PH.D.

As of 2010, 13 percent of the population was age 65 and older, with this group expected to comprise 19.3 percent of the population by 2030.[1] Elder abuse among this population is both a pervasive problem and a growing concern.[2] Given that the vast majority (96.9 percent) of older Americans are residing in domestic settings,[3] it is not surprising that the majority (89.3 percent) of elder abuse reported to Adult Protective Services (APS) occurs in domestic settings.[4] And yet, although greater recognition of the occurrence of elder abuse is beginning to emerge, the field has generated few theory-based explanations of what causes elder abuse and how best to respond to it. This paper reports the findings of two studies funded by the National Institute of Justice (NIJ) in an effort to begin to fill this void. The theoretical directions suggested in this paper are intended to spur the critique of existing theories and facilitate the development of new theories that will enhance our understanding of elder abuse. This paper addresses only a subset of the various types of elder abuse; future work should attend to other forms of elder maltreatment (e.g., psychological, sexual) not addressed here.

## The Purpose and Role of Theory in Science

A theory provides an explanation of some aspect of the surrounding world and answers the question of why something happens the way it does.[5] As William James might say, it is an attempt to make sense of the "humming-buzzing confusion" in which we live.[6] In addition to enhancing understanding of a phenomenon, a theory, at its core, provides coherence to a disparate, yet nonetheless related, set of variables; identifies factors that should be included in explanatory models; and facilitates the interpretation of observations and research results. Progress in science necessitates that testable hypotheses be generated from a theory, with these hypotheses, in turn, empirically examined. The results of this examination are then used to assess the reliability and validity of the theory's predictions and, ultimately, the theory itself (see Figure 1). This process should be replicated over time, which will result in some theories being rejected and discarded, others amended, and new theories being created where needed.

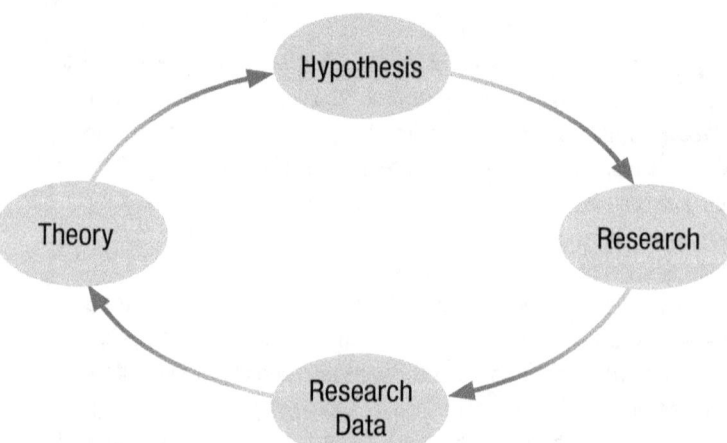

Figure 1. The Cyclical Relationship Between Research and Theory.

Needless to say, theory evaluation is closely related to theory development. Theory evaluation is based on five generally accepted criteria.[7] First is the principle of parsimony, which contends that the selection among competing hypotheses should be based on which one requires the fewest assumptions and thereby offers the simplest explanation of a phenomenon. Theories that have a simpler foundation are preferable to complex articulations where there are more assumptions that may later prove invalid or obfuscate understanding of the underlying phenomenon. For example, Sacco argues that the construct of elder abuse fails the test of parsimony because there are more fundamental rubrics under which elder abuse might exist.[8] Thus, the abuse of elderly individuals by their adult children could be framed instead within a broader parental abuse paradigm.[9]

Second, a theory should have high explanatory value accounting for as much conceptual and empirical variation as possible. For example, elder abuse theories become more valuable if they account for not only the elderly victims but also the abusive individuals involved and the specific context within which the abuse takes place.

Third, the theory must be testable. Thus, key concepts such as the "abuse" in "elder abuse" must be capable of being operationally defined and measured, as well as who is considered to be an "elderly" person for this purpose.

Fourth, a theory should be novel. It should offer ideas about elder abuse that better explain its occurrence than previously available explanations and should advance our understanding of it. For example, the caregiver stress model,[10] which had long been the predominant theory used to explain the underlying dynamics of elder abuse, was in turn supplemented by other theories, such as the family violence model.[11]

Finally, the validity and reliability of a theory are critical, which addresses the extent to which the hypotheses generated by a theory match empirical observations of the underlying phenomena and are replicable over time and across studies. For example, a theory that asserts elder abuse is generally committed by someone who is a virtual stranger to the elderly person is inconsistent with multiple findings that elder abuse is predominantly committed by family members and others who are well known to the victim.[12]

## Elder Abuse Understanding and Research Has Been Largely Devoid of Guiding Theory

In the initial development of an emerging field, there is typically an overabundance of theory and an absence of systematic empirical research. This was the case with regard to child maltreatment, where published theory papers predominated at first (see Figure 2), guiding subsequent empirical research and related papers. Over time, as quantitative data accumulate and agreement regarding explanatory principles coalesces, less attention tends to be given to underlying theory, and fewer related papers tend to be published.[13]

However, this has not been the pattern with regard to elder abuse. Elder abuse lags behind other areas of family violence in theory development,[14] although this may be in part because less attention has been devoted to elder abuse

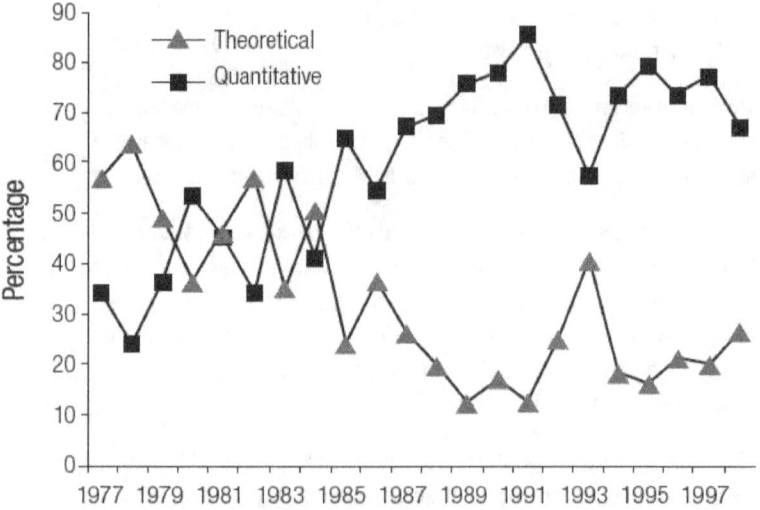

Figure 2. The Change in Frequency of Theoretical Articles Compared with Quantitative Articles in the Field of Child Maltreatment Over Time.

Source: Behl, L.E., H.A. Conyngham, and P.F. May, "Trends in Child Maltreatment Literature," Child Abuse & Neglect, 27 (2) (2003): 215–229, doi:10.1016/j.chiabu.2003.10.001.

in general, which explains why the field has produced a smaller number of peer-reviewed publications. Indeed, the field of elder abuse has been criticized for failing to develop theory that adequately and specifically addresses elder maltreatment.[15] The theories that do exist have been adapted from other fields.

## Possible Explanations for Why the Field Has Been Largely Devoid of Guiding Theory

There are several explanations for why the field of elder abuse has been devoid of guiding theory. These include the fact that elder abuse has received little national attention and concern, limited recognition at the federal level and a lack of funding to support theory development, and the field has tended to rely heavily on a presumption that the caregiver stress model provides a full explanation of the occurrence of elder abuse. Each of these is discussed in greater detail below.

**Elder abuse lacks national attention and concern.** Elder abuse has not gained the same national notoriety that would elevate it to an urgent social problem and coalesce support for addressing it as other forms of family violence have achieved, primarily because no powerful group has taken up this issue as its cause. Child maltreatment was propelled onto the national stage by professional organizations such as the American Medical Association and family physicians,[16] while intimate partner violence (IPV) was propelled into the public sphere by grassroots organizations associated with the women's movement and concern about the prevalence and harm of IPV.[17] However, no powerful advocacy group has similarly taken up the gauntlet for elder abuse. Although the publication of high national incidence and prevalence rates could propel this social problem into the national spotlight, the field has been devoid of such studies until very recently[18] and continues to lack a national data collection system. Without these data or some other means of understanding the existence and prevalence of elder abuse, society will fail to respond. In addition, ageism may contribute to this phenomenon, as negative attitudes toward elderly people can contribute to apathy toward their mistreatment and help account for the absence of a "moral panic" regarding the abuse of the elderly.[19] Finally, although the potential exists for older Americans as a group to take up this cause, it is a misconception that they routinely vote as a political bloc.[20]

**Elder abuse has received little federal recognition and funding to combat it.** Compared with child maltreatment and IPV, elder abuse has been the focus of little federal policy or funding. Elder abuse has suffered from a lack of legislation and preventive and remedial funding; elder abuse research and data collection efforts; and national, state and local consensus statements and policy directives. Congress passed the Child Abuse Prevention and Treatment Act (CAPTA) in 1974 (P.L. 93-247) and the Violence against Women Act (VAWA) in 1994 (P.L. 103-322). Only in 2010 did Congress pass the Elder Justice Act (P.L. 111-148), and even then it was not accompanied by an appropriation of funding.

The lack of national attention to elder abuse has very real implications for efforts to address elder abuse. Without dedicated advocacy and a widespread sense of urgency, legislators faced with a host of competing demands and limited funds are more likely to target resources to those issues that have been made a high priority by their constituents. Indeed, elder abuse research has been severely underfunded and lags behind other forms of family violence. Although NIJ has substantially increased its funding for elder abuse research in recent years, for every dollar of federal funding apportioned to family violence, 97 cents is apportioned to child maltreatment, 2 cents is devoted to IPV, and 1 cent is spent on elder abuse.[21]

**Elder abuse remains focused predominantly on the caregiver stress model.** APS, the collection of state agencies that have been charged with responding to elder abuse, is guided primarily by the caregiver stress model that once dominated the field.[22] This model is premised on the belief that elder abuse can be attributed to the stress associated with providing care and assistance to frail and highly dependent elderly people.[23] Although the initial adoption of this model is understandable given the historical context in which APS was developed,[24] its continued use may be limiting the development of better alternative or supplemental explanatory models. The caregiver stress model has recently fallen out of favor among many scholars.[25] When a field relies on outdated perceptions (either out of fear of offending the status quo or because funding sources insist on a deferral to the status quo), efforts to generate alternative hypotheses that might better explain a given phenomenon suffer.[26]

## Review of Existing Theories

As mentioned, rather than developing theories unique to elder abuse, scholars have tended to adopt or adapt existing theories from other fields.[27] Recently, Burnight and Mosqueda systematically reviewed seven elder abuse theories.[28] An emphasis on interpersonal relationships was found to be the predominant focus of existing theory-building in this field, although other applications involved sociocultural, multisystemic and sociocultural contextual approaches. A brief summary of each theory and its possible application to elder abuse is presented below.

One interpersonal approach, the Caregiver Stress Theory, asserts that parents experiencing stress are more likely to maltreat their children.[29] In the context of elder maltreatment, it has been posited that maltreatment occurs when family members caring for an impaired older adult are unable to adequately manage their caregiving responsibilities.[30] The elderly victim is typically described as highly dependent on the caregiver, who becomes overwhelmed, frustrated and abusive because of the continuous caretaking demands posed by the elderly person.

Another interpersonal approach, the Social Learning Theory, posits that violent acts are a learned behavior transferred through the process of modeling.[31] This theory was developed to explain violent behavior in children and has been used extensively to account for child maltreatment and IPV. Elder abuse is posited as the result of the abusive individual having learned to use violence in an earlier context to either resolve conflicts or obtain a desired outcome. The theory has also been called the Cycle of Violence Model and the Intergenerational Transmission of Violence Model.[32]

The Social Exchange Theory, a third interpersonal approach, is rooted in psychology and economics. It conceptualizes social behavior as involving negotiated exchanges of material and nonmaterial goods and services.[33] In the context of family violence, the theory has been used predominantly to explain IPV. Decalmer and Glendenning contend that, pursuant to the theory's tenets, when the sociodynamic balance in a relationship is upset or perceived to have been upset, the disadvantaged party will use violence to restore balance.[34] As applied to elder abuse, abusive individuals are postulated to perceive themselves as not receiving their fair share from their relationship with the elderly person or other family members, and their resort to violence is an effort to restore or obtain deserved equilibrium.

The Background-Situational Theory (Dyadic Discord Theory), also an interpersonal approach, asserts that relationship discord results from a combination of contextual factors (e.g., a history of family violence, which primes a person's acceptance of violence as a conflict resolution strategy) and situational factors (e.g., a lack of relationship satisfaction).[35] The theory has been used predominately to explain courtship violence.[36] It can readily be applied to elder abuse when the abusive individual is the spouse or intimate partner of the victim, but it might also apply when the abusive individual is a codependent adult child or caregiver of the elderly person.

A sociocultural (feminist) approach, the Power and Control Theory, highlights an abusive individual's use of a pattern of coercive tactics to gain and maintain power and control during the course of a relationship with another person.[37] This theory has been used extensively to explain IPV.[38] Brandl has adopted this theory to explain spousal abuse among elderly couples, although it could be applied as well when such traits describe an adult child or caregiver who has assumed, perhaps grudgingly, responsibility for the elderly person.[39]

A multisystemic approach, the Ecological Model originally sought to explain human development by including a range of potential influences on this process, including the impact of individual, relationship, community and societal influences.[40] This model has been applied in conjunction with IPV to encompass a diverse range of potential causes of abuse.[41] More recently, the theory has been adapted to identify a large number of factors pertaining to elder maltreatment that arise through individual, relationship, community and societal influences.[42]

Finally, a sociocultural contextual approach, the Biopsychosocial Model, was introduced by Engel to correct for limitations resulting from the application of the biomedical model employed predominantly by the health care system at that time and argued that social as well as biomedical factors contributed to illness.[43] Drawing inspiration from Engel,[44] Bonnie and Wallace proposed the use of this model as a foundation for elder maltreatment theory.[45] Under this theory, elder maltreatment can be attributed to the characteristics of both the elderly person and the abusive individual, both of whom are embedded in a larger sociocultural context (family and friends); their status inequality, relationship type, and power and exchange dynamics should all be taken into account.[46]

## The Absence of a Critical Examination and Testing of Existing Theories

Although a listing of existing theories is useful, these theories have not been adequately tested or critiqued, and none of them has been systematically critiqued with the five widely accepted criteria described above for evaluating theories.

**Absence of critical examination.** For example, although the social exchange theory has frequently been used in recent years to explain elder abuse,[47] Jackson and Hafemeister suggest that this theory may have limited application when explaining the continuation of abuse involving elderly parents and their adult offspring,[48] which some studies suggest is the most common dyad in elder abuse cases.[49]

The social exchange model posits that for a relationship to be harmonious and extended, it needs to be balanced for the various parties involved in terms of its costs (e.g., the time and effort put into the relationship) and benefits (e.g., the rewards and satisfaction obtained from the relationship). When one of the parties perceives an imbalance, discord is expected to result; if the imbalance becomes too great, the model anticipates that violence will erupt and the relationship may be severed.

Although it may have considerable explanatory value when addressing the smoldering resentment felt by relatively independent spouses in a relationship and the conflict's outcome, the social exchange theory may be less applicable to situations involving parents and adult offspring, particularly when they have become dependent — physically, financially or emotionally — upon one another. In cases of elder abuse by an adult offspring, the abused parent, often a mother, will in many cases have been expending tremendous energy and incurring other substantial costs providing care for the adult offspring, who may be dependent upon his or her parent because of financial needs, a serious mental illness, or substance abuse disorder.[50] The social exchange theory would predict that the abused elderly parent, who is generally receiving little apparent benefit from the adult offspring, would become dissatisfied with the relationship and readily seek and welcome an end to the relationship. However, these elderly parents often do not follow this path, perhaps reflecting an overriding personal or societal norm of continuing parental affection, attachment and obligation.[51] There also may be cases in which the elderly parent is physically incapable of leaving the situation or may fear institutional placement if the dyad is separated.[52] In cases involving elderly parents and adult offspring, the use of the social exchange theory would result in erroneous predictions and beliefs about the course of elder abuse.

**Absence of adequate testing of existing theories.** Although adopting or adapting existing theories from other fields can be an efficient approach, the resulting theories must be tested for validity and reliability within the new context. The lack of such testing has been particularly pervasive with regard to these emerging models of elder abuse. One characteristic of the pervasive lack of model testing has been to use these models to explain all types of elder abuse. For example, in recent years there have been numerous attempts to universally apply theories that explain family violence. However, financial exploitation of the elderly — which is often cited as the fastest-growing form of elder abuse, with 33 percent or more of elder abuse cases involving financial abuse[53] — is perpetrated relatively equally by family and nonfamily members.[54] Therefore, a family violence framework would have, at best, limited applicability to this sizeable set of elder abuse cases. Pittaway, Westhues and Peressini used a large, nationally representative Canadian sample of victims to test the application of variables associated with family violence to elder abuse and determined that the variables typically associated with family violence did not explain financial exploitation.[55]

Similarly, Jackson and Hafemeister recently identified important differences when financial exploitation co-occurs with physical abuse and/or neglect.[56]

For example, financial exploitation that does not co-occur with physical abuse or neglect is perpetrated by both family and nonfamily members, whereas "hybrid" financial exploitation (i.e., financial exploitation co-occurring with physical abuse and/or neglect) involved only family members. A theory traditionally used to explain family violence may be appropriate for explaining hybrid financial exploitation but not for "pure" financial exploitation, which may have more in common with white collar crime.[57]

The application of the various theoretical models borrowed from other domains to elder abuse requires this kind of nuanced critique and testing. An initial assessment suggests that these theories do not always fit well or may be applied too broadly and not be well suited for explaining various aspects of elder abuse, and in turn may result in many key points and insights being missed or, worse, promotion of inaccurate beliefs and assumptions.

## Explanations for Why Existing Theories Have Tended to Be a Poor or Limited Fit

Concurrent with the Burnight and Mosqueda study,[58] Jackson and Hafemeister undertook a review of existing models' ability to provide theory-based explanations for their research findings regarding elder abuse.[59] Theories included those from the fields of psychology,[60] phenomenology,[61] aging,[62] criminology[63] and sociology,[64] as well as feminist theories[65] and ecological models.[66] However, none of the models fully explained the underlying empirical data, leading the authors to explore why existing theory failed to adequately explain their findings.[67] Jackson and Hafemeister reached a series of determinations.

The first limitation that the authors recognized was the fact that elder abuse tends to be multidimensional, with a significant number of factors contributing to its occurrence and considerable variation existing across the different types of elder abuse. One criticism of the current approach to theory development in this field that seems warranted is a tendency toward overinclusion and lumping all forms of elder maltreatment together within a single theoretical model.[68] Existing theories tend to treat elder abuse as a monolithic phenomenon,[69] although it clearly seems to consist of a number of relatively disparate and unrelated sets of events. Bonnie and Wallace went so far as to conjecture that the different types of elder abuse "may be basically independent."[70]

Second, the field has tended to focus on either the victims or the abusive individuals, failing to take into consideration that both, in the course of their relationship, play a role in the occurrence of elder abuse — which is not to say they are equally to blame for this abuse. A focus on only one or the other results in an incomplete understanding of the phenomenon.[71] For example, a psychopathology model focuses only on the abusive individual, with little regard given to the role played by the victim — in this case the elderly person — and thus fails to capture the complacency or even the tacit complicity of some victims.[72] It should be acknowledged that not all elderly people are "pure victims."[73]

Similarly, not all abusive individuals are driven by evil intent and malicious motives. For example, in cases of financial exploitation, the abusive individual may simply have failed to resist an unexpected opportunity. Alternatively, in cases of neglect, the caretaker may have been distracted, overwhelmed or insufficiently attentive to the needs of an elderly person for whose welfare they were responsible. In cases of physical abuse, an attack may reflect the culmination of a cycle of escalating violence to which both parties contributed. While not excusable, such behavior does not fall within the range of what is generally referred to as psychopathological behavior.[74]

Relatedly, failure to take the relationship between the elderly victim and the abusive individual into consideration can lead to inapplicable theories. For example, there are often different dynamics involved when a family member financially exploits an elderly person and when a stranger does.[75] Understanding the dynamics of the dyadic relationship involved is generally critical to understanding and explaining the nature of the elder abuse and responding appropriately to it.

Finally, despite widespread calls for a multidisciplinary approach to the study of elder abuse, theorists in this field have tended to stay within their narrowly defined domains or disciplines,[76] although a theory drawn from a single discipline is likely to miss important aspects of the complexity, diversity and uniqueness of elder abuse.

## Future Directions

To address these shortcomings, several adjustments should be made. First, the practice of treating elder abuse as a monolithic phenomenon should be discarded and replaced with a recognition that elder maltreatment can take several different forms and that the nature of the abuse varies with the type of maltreatment involved. Second, theories should include factors pertaining to both the victim and the abusive individual. Third, the nature of the relationship that brings these parties together, and the context in which that relationship arises, should be taken into account. Each of these adjustments is discussed in greater detail below.

**Elder abuse is not a monolithic phenomenon.** As noted, theorists have historically treated elder abuse as a monolithic phenomenon. However, Jackson and Hafemeister, focusing on physical abuse, neglect, pure financial exploitation and hybrid financial exploitation, found that the characteristics of the victim and the abusive individual, the nature of their relationship and occurring abuse, and the triggering factors and appropriate response varied with the type of maltreatment involved, strongly indicating that one theory will not adequately address "elder maltreatment."[77]

*Type of maltreatment.* Jackson and Hafemeister used two data sets to determine whether and how four forms of elder maltreatment differed. One data source consisted of interviews with 71 APS caseworkers, 55 of their elderly clients for whom there had been a substantiated disposition of elder abuse, and 35 third-party informants (someone other than the abusive individual who was familiar with the situation).[78] The types of abuse included financial exploitation (n = 38), physical abuse (n = 8), neglect by other (n = 9) and hybrid financial exploitation (n = 16). The other data source was the Adult Services/Adult Protective Services (ASAPS) database maintained by the Virginia Department of Social Services. At the close of every case, APS caseworkers enter case data into ASAPS. This statewide database was accessed for variables that mirrored the interview data and covered a comparable two-year period. From the 165 items available in the ASAPS database, 40 were selected for inclusion as independent and dependent variables. Only those cases involving financial exploitation (n = 472), physical abuse (n = 332), neglect by other (n = 1,176) and hybrid financial exploitation (n = 162) were included, resulting in the identification of 2,142 substantiated cases of elder abuse.

Jackson and Hafemeister found pronounced differences across these four types of elder maltreatment with regard to victim and abusive individual risk factors,[79] case characteristics,[80] interpersonal dynamics[81] and outcomes.[82]

As mentioned, an attempt was made to identify a theoretical model that would explain these results.[83] Because none of the existing theories provided an adequate explanation, an effort was undertaken to develop new or adapt existing theories.[84] This effort began with two basic premises. First, because of the differences found among the various types of elder abuse studied (pure financial exploitation, physical abuse, neglect and hybrid financial exploitation), it was postulated that a separate theoretical model may be necessary for each type of elder maltreatment. Second, because the behavior and motivations of both the elderly person and the abusive individual varied with the type of elder abuse involved, the respective theoretical models should be prepared to take into account factors associated with both parties. The resulting theories have yet to be tested, but their articulation is intended to help improve our theory-based understanding of elder abuse by generating testable hypotheses and suggesting new lines of research. The results are briefly described below.[85]

*Pure financial exploitation.* Financially exploited elderly people experienced a range of financial crimes and misdeeds, including theft, fraud and misuse of their assets.[86] These victims often lack someone with whom they can consult or who will monitor their financial activities, may be particularly trusting of others in part because they were treated well as children, may be experiencing an emerging and relatively unrecognized cognitive impairment, and are often very worried about a possible future loss of independence, any of which may enable someone to take advantage of and financially exploit the elderly person.

*Physical abuse.* Physical abuse of an elderly person typically involves a family member, often an adult offspring. Contrary to previous beliefs, data show that many elderly victims of physical abuse are relatively high-functioning individuals who may be providing long-term support to adult offspring or other family members, who in turn may be dependent on and abusive toward the elderly person.[87] Although the elderly person is generally aware that he or she is being mistreated and has resulting feelings of ambivalence toward the abusive individuals, the feelings of parental or familial obligation tend to trump thoughts of severing the relationship. The violence often stems from the abusive individual's resentment at their dependence on the elderly person, as well as the close proximity, continuing interactions and ongoing friction. A history of dependency may sensitize the abusive individual to perceived criticisms and "attacks" from the elderly person, enhancing the likelihood of a violent response.

*Neglect.* Typically, neglect occurs when vulnerable elderly people are being cared for by individuals who fail to adequately fulfill their responsibility. When family members fail to fulfill this responsibility, the elderly victims may acknowledge that they were not stellar parents when these family members were young, with the abusive individual now figuratively saying, "You weren't there for me when I was young, and I'm not going to be here for you now." Thus, attachment theory may help explain why a small proportion of adult offspring neglect their elderly parents, as these individuals may have been insecurely attached to their parents as young children, minimizing their feelings of affinity and filial obligation now that the elderly parent is in need of their assistance. It must be recognized that there are cases in which someone is simply incapable of caring for an elderly parent due to the person's own physical or cognitive limitations, but such cases are less likely to be designated as elder abuse by APS.

*Hybrid financial exploitation.* It has been determined that a relatively unrecognized scenario, referred to as hybrid financial exploitation, arises when financial exploitation co-occurs with physical abuse and/or neglect.[88] These cases typically involve financially dependent family members, particularly adult offspring, who have been cared for by the elderly person for years, if not decades. The abuse suffered by these elderly victims is frequently longstanding. Over time, however, as the elderly person's health declines and the elderly person becomes more socially isolated, often as the result of the death of a spouse, the elderly person increasingly becomes more dependent on another family member for care, resulting in a mutual dependency, albeit with each member of the dyad experiencing a different type of dependency. Although sharing some features in common with physical abuse and neglect, hybrid financial exploitation cases are unique in many ways and tend to result in worse outcomes for elderly victims than result from other forms of elder maltreatment.[89] These outcomes may be attributable to the additional stress associated with the financial loss that is experienced.

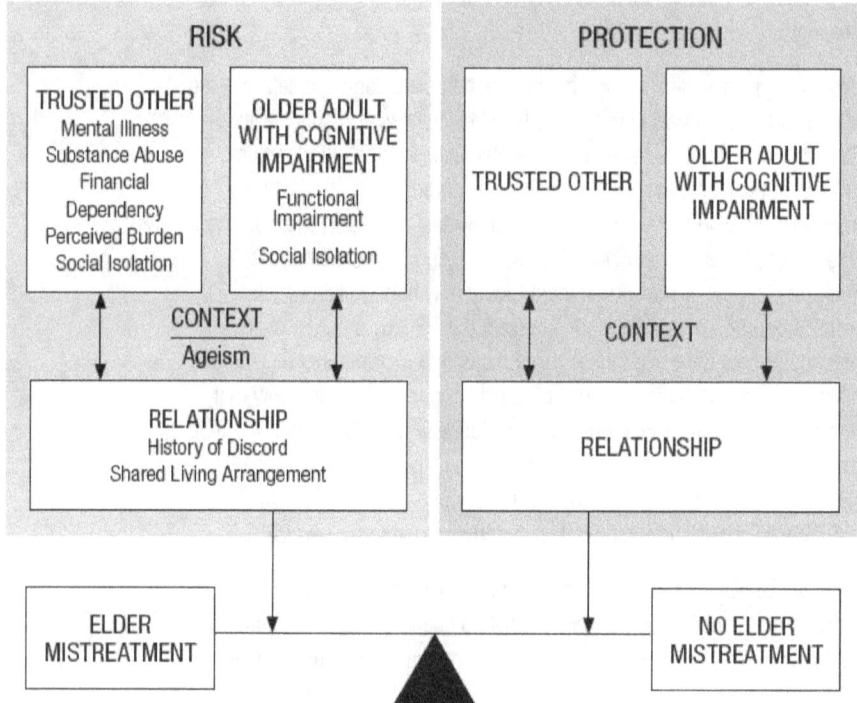

Figure 3. A Risk-Protection Model of Elder Mistreatment of Older Adults with Cognitive Impairment

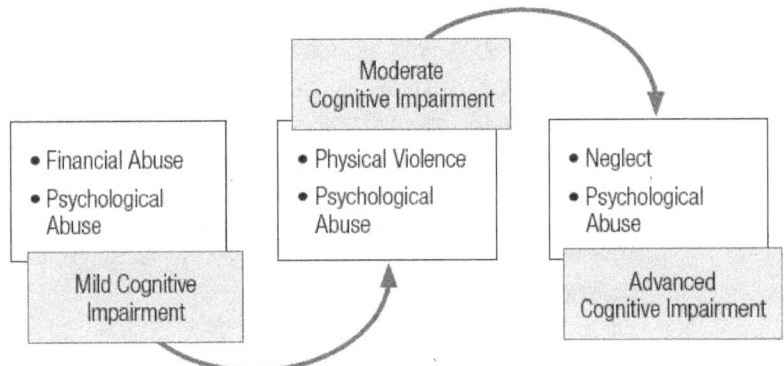

Figure 4. Elder Mistreatment in Older Adults in Different Stages of Cognitive Impairment

*Cognitive impairment.* Beyond distinguishing the type of abuse involved, there are a number of other ways in which elder abuse may be analyzed to gain a more accurate understanding. For example, Burnight and Mosqueda suggest that elder abuse can be categorized in part by whether the elderly person has a cognitive impairment.[90] This approach integrates a number of existing theories, including the dyadic discord theory, the power and control theory, the social exchange theory, the caregiver stress theory, and the ecological model. It focuses on the risk-enhancing and protective factors associated with being a cognitively impaired elderly person, the involvement of a "trusted other" on whom the elderly person relies, the context in which they live, and the nature of their relationship (see Figure 3). Using existing research, Burnight and Mosqueda have identified several factors that enhance the risk of elder abuse when an elderly person is cognitively impaired. However, they have also noted that the literature has failed to identify countervailing factors in these circumstances, although the presence of these factors may be critical in preventing elder mistreatment. A resulting Risk-Protection Model could generate a number of valuable testable hypotheses. For example, maintaining the social connections of cognitively impaired elderly people may provide a protective factor that lowers the incidence of elder mistreatment.

Burnight and Mosqueda also hypothesize that the type of abuse to which an elderly person with a cognitive impairment is most subject will vary with the severity of the impairment.[91] As shown in Figure 4, during early dementia, financial exploitation may be a greater risk than physical violence or neglect. As the dementia progresses to a moderate impairment, the elderly person may become particularly vulnerable to physical abuse. In the advanced stages of dementia, neglect may be the most likely of these three types of elder maltreatment. While intriguing, this model awaits further testing.

**A dynamic approach that encompasses both the elderly victim and the abusive individual should be used.** Initially, the field was focused primarily on the victims of elder abuse.[92] The psychopathology model reversed this trend by emphasizing the role of the abusive individual.[93] However, research shows that characteristics of both the victim and the abusive individual predict the occurrence of different forms of elder maltreatment.[94] These findings suggest that theoretical models of elder abuse must take into consideration both parties in these dyadic relationships.[95] The field should move away from a relatively narrow approach that concentrates on only one party or the other and evolve toward a more dynamic approach that seeks to understand the interactions between these two parties and what drives and motivates them. Doing so will require a paradigm shift[96] away from the APS model, which tends to focus exclusively on the victims of elder abuse and their need for services,[97] and the criminal justice system approach, with its singular focus on punishing the abusive individual, toward a more integrated approach.[98]

Explicitly incorporate the nature of the relationship between the elderly victim and the abusive individual. Even after distinguishing among the different types of maltreatment, taking into account the victim's cognitive status and embracing a dynamic conceptualization of elder maltreatment, further subtleties may need to be identified — such as the nature of the relationship between the elderly victim and the abusive individual — to gain the necessary understanding of elder abuse. For example, a distinct dynamic may arise when the abusive individual is a family member.[99] As noted above, one of the challenges associated with developing a theoretical model for financial exploitation is the heterogeneity of the nature of the relationships between the elderly people and the abusive individuals.[100] Because sometimes the individuals involved are related and sometimes they are virtual strangers, the motivations of the involved parties can vary enormously.[101] Similarly, the nature of the relationship can vary enormously depending on the elderly person's age, health, mental capabilities, availability of support systems and relationships with (other) family members and other people in the community, factors that may vary considerably between elderly individuals.[102]

In addition, the myriad ways in which an elderly person may be financially exploited[103] increase the complexity of theory development, particularly depending on whether force or threat was involved or whether guile and deception was used. Therefore, even within a given type of abuse, such as financial exploitation, it may be necessary to develop different theories to explain the various subtypes of abuse.[104]

## The Theory, Research and Intervention Triangle

To develop the needed theory-based foundations to promote understanding of elder abuse and facilitate the identification of means to prevent this abuse and respond appropriately when it does take place, a confluence of theory, research and practice must occur. This can only happen when the following steps are taken.

**Funding must be made available to support needed research.** Although theory may be developed initially in the absence of empirical data, eventually there is a need for empirical validation of a theory and its predictions, which in turn will provide an empirical foundation upon which to expand or modify existing theories. The development of theory and research relevant to elder abuse has been hampered by a lack of supporting state and federal funding. If society is to respond appropriately and adequately to elder abuse, sufficient funding must be made available to develop the needed scientific foundation. To achieve this goal, it will be necessary for at least one group, and hopefully multiple groups, to take up the "cause" of elder abuse and elevate it to a social problem worthy of funding to understand it better.

**Increased availability of clinical and nationally representative samples for study.** Gaining access to elderly victims for research purposes is challenging under the best of circumstances, but without the assistance of practitioners who routinely work with this population, such as physicians, other clinicians, APS caseworkers, law enforcement officials and prosecutors, this research is almost impossible to conduct. Two useful documents have been developed to enhance the occurrence of this critical research. The documents, produced by the National Adult Protective Services Association and the National Committee for the Prevention of Elder Abuse Research Committee, attempt to enhance working relationships between researchers and APS.[105] Similar guidance needs to be developed to facilitate interactions between researchers and other relevant practitioners.

As is typical with nascent fields, most research has been conducted using relatively small samples, such as may be obtained through a given APS agency. Although this can be a reasonable approach depending on the question being asked, there is a need for nationally representative studies, particularly because only between 1 in 23 and 1 in 14 cases of elder abuse comes to the attention of the agencies formally authorized to respond to them, such as APS or law enforcement. [106, 107] There may be important differences between clinical and nationally representative samples, as has been found in other fields,[108] with important implications for the derived development of theory.

**The stakes are too high for researchers to get it wrong.** Theory development pertaining to elder abuse is not just an academic exercise but may have critical implications for victim safety. Interventions to promote and enhance victim safety are drawn directly from our conceptualization of the underlying problem.[109] The stakes are simply too high for the theory upon which the intervention is based to be wrong. It is widely acknowledged that the initial demonstration projects undertaken 40 years ago ended up providing little assistance and protection for elderly people,[110] likely because the interventions were based upon incorrect theoretical assumptions. Similarly, recent research has shown that many of the interventions employed currently are relatively ineffective and sometimes even counterproductive,[111] perhaps because they continue to suffer from faulty theoretical foundations.[112]

Appropriate protective and intervention programs are urgently needed to respond to and protect the growing population of elderly people in our society.[113] To succeed, these programs must be based on sound theory and then systematically evaluated using scientific methods.[114] For example, the recognition that elder abuse typically involves a dynamic relationship between the elderly victim and the abusive individual suggests that appropriate interventions should target both parties.[115]

## Conclusions

The response to elder maltreatment needs to change from a relatively fragmented approach unguided by theory to one that embraces a systematic approach drawn from a greater understanding of the underlying phenomenon. Further, these theories should take into account the characteristics of both the elderly victims and the abusive individuals, including their cognitive statuses, the nature of their relationships, the settings in which the abuse occurs, the type of abuse involved, and protective factors; in general, the theories should employ a more dynamic approach. Researchers should then test the resulting constructs, including the tenets presented in this article, and help build a foundation that will both deepen our understanding of elder maltreatment and form a basis for crafting more effective interventions to increase the safety and well-being of elderly people.

[1] Werner, C.A., "The Older Population: 2010," 2010 Census Briefs (C2010BR-09), Washington, D.C.: U.S. Census Bureau, November 2011, retrieved April 10, 2013, from http://www.census.gov/prod/cen2010/briefs/c2010br-09.pdf.

[2] Acierno, R., M.A. Hernandez, A.B. Amstadter, H.S. Resnick, K. Steve, W. Muzzy, and D.G. Kilpatrick, "Prevalence and Correlates of Emotional, Physical, Sexual, and Financial Abuse and Potential Neglect in the United States: The National Elder Mistreatment Study," American Journal of Public Health 100 (2) (2010): 292–297; Bonnie, R.L., and R.B. Wallace, eds., Elder Mistreatment: Abuse, Neglect, and Exploitation in an Aging America. Washington, D.C.: The National Academies Press, 2003; Cooper, C., A. Selwood, and G. Livingston, "The Prevalence of Elder Abuse and Neglect: A Systematic Review," Age & Ageing, 37 (2008): 151–160; Lachs, M.S., and J. Berman, Under the Radar: New York State Elder Abuse Prevalence Study, Rensselaer, N.Y.: William B. Hoyt Memorial New York State Children, Family Trust Fund, New York State Office of Children and Family Services, 2011; Laumann, E.O., S.A. Leitsch, and L.J. Waite, "Elder Mistreatment in the United States: Prevalence Estimates From a Nationally Representative Study," Journal of Gerontology, 63 (2008): 48–54.

[3] Werner, 2010.

[4] Teaster, P., T. Dugar, M. Mendiondo, E. Abner, K. Cecil, and J. Otto, The 2004 Survey of State Adult Protective Services: Abuse of Adults 60 Years of Age and Older, Washington D.C.: National Center on Elder Abuse, 2006.

[5] Brownstein, H., M.A. Zahn, and S.L. Jackson, "Introduction," in Violence: From Theory to Research, eds. M.A. Zahn, H. Brownstein, and S.L. Jackson, San Francisco, Calif.: Anderson Lexis Nexis, 2004: 1–14.

[6] James, W., Essays in Radical Empiricism, New York: Longmans, Green & Company, 1912.

[7] Brownstein, Zahn, and Jackson, 2004.

[8] Sacco, V.F., "Conceptualizing Elder Abuse: Implications for Research and Theory," in Fear of Crime and Criminal Victimization, eds. W. Bilsky, C. Pfeiffer, and P. Wetzels, Stuttgart, Germany: Verlag, 1993: 71–82.

[9] For a review see, e.g., Kennair, N., & D. Mellor, "Parent Abuse: A Review," Child Psychiatry & Human Development, 38 (2007): 203–219.

[10]Steinmetz, S.K., "Battered Parents," Society, 15 (5) (1978): 54–55, doi:10.1007/bf02701616.

[11]Pillemer, K., "Elder Abuse Is Caused by the Deviance and Dependence of Abusive Caregivers," in Current Controversies on Family Violence, 2nd ed., eds. D.R. Loseke, R.J. Gelles, and M.M. Cavanaugh, Thousand Oaks, Calif.: Sage, 2005: 207–220.

[12]Jackson, S.L., and T.L. Hafemeister, "Risk Factors Associated with Elder Abuse: The Importance of Differentiating by Type of Elder Maltreatment," Violence & Victims, 26 (6) (2011): 738–757; Teaster et al., 2006.

[13]Behl, L.E., H.A. Conyngham, and P.F. May, "Trends in Child Maltreatment Literature," Child Abuse & Neglect, 27 (2) (2003): 215–229, doi:10.1016/j.chiabu.2003.10.001.

[14]Tolan, P., D. Gorman-Smith, and D. Henry, "Family Violence," Annual Review of Psychology, 57 (2006): 557–583; World Health Organization, World Report on Violence and Health: Summary, Geneva, Switzerland: Author, 2002.

[15]Bonnie and Wallace, 2003; Lowenstein, A., "Elder Abuse and Neglect – 'Old Phenomenon': New Directions for Research, Legislation, and Service Developments," Journal of Elder Abuse & Neglect, 21 (2009): 278–287; Anetzberger, G.J., "An Update on the Nature and Scope of Elder Abuse," Generations, 36 (3) (2012): 12–20.

[16]Hafemeister, T.L., "Castles Made of Sand? Rediscovering Child Abuse and Society's Response," Ohio Northern University Law Review, 36 (2010): 819–913; Kempe, C.H., F.N. Silverman, B.F. Steele, W. Droegemueller, and H.K. Silver, "The Battered-Child Syndrome," JAMA, 181 (1962): 17–24.

[17]Hafemeister, T.L., "If All You Have Is a Hammer: Society's Ineffective Response to Intimate Partner Violence," Catholic University Law Review, 60 (1) (2011): 919–1001; Laney, G.P., Violence Against Women Act: History and Federal Funding, Washington, D.C.: Congressional Research Service, 2011, available at http://digitalcommons.ilr.cornell.edu/key_workplace/711.

[18]Acierno et al., 2010; Laumann, Leitsch, and Waite, 2008.

[19]Nelson, T.D., "Ageism: Prejudice Against Our Feared Future Self," Journal of Social Issues, 61 (2) (2005): 207–221; Penhale, B., and P. Kingston, "Social Perspectives on Elder Abuse, in Family Violence and the

Caring Professions, eds., P. Kingston and B. Penhale, London: Macmillan, 1995: 222–244; Phelan, A., "Elder Abuse, Ageism, and Human Rights and Citizenship: Implications for Nursing Discourse," Nursing Inquiry, 15 (4) (2008): 320–329.

[20]Binstock, R.H., "Old-Age Policies, Politics, and Ageism," Generations, 29 (3) (2005): 73–78; Butler, R.N., "Age-Ism: Another Form of Bigotry," The Gerontologist, 9 (1969): 243–246.

[21]Quinn, K., Closing plenary session at the 17th annual conference of the Virginia Coalition for the Prevention of Elder Abuse, Virginia Beach, Va., June 2011.

[22]Quinn, K., and H. Zielke, "Elder Abuse, Neglect, and Exploitation: Policy Issues," Clinics in Geriatric Medicine, 21 (2005): 449–457.

[23]Nerenberg, L., Preventing Elder Abuse by Family Caregivers, Washington, D.C.: National Center on Elder Abuse, 2002.

[24]Quinn and Zielke, 2005.

[25]Anetzberger, G.J., "Caregiving: Primary Cause of Elder Abuse?," Generations, 24 (2) (2000): 46–51; Benson, W.F., "Tales from the Elder Justice Act and Other Stories of Life Inside the Beltway," remarks presented at the annual conference of the Virginia Coalition for the Prevention of Elder Abuse, Virginia Beach, Va., 2008; Bergeron, L.R., "An Elder Abuse Case Study: Caregiver Stress or Domestic Violence? You Decide," Journal of Gerontological Social Work, 34 (2001): 47–63; Bonnie and Wallace, 2003; Brandl, B., and D.L. Horan, "Domestic Violence in Later Life: An Overview for Health Care Providers," in Domestic Violence and Health Care: Policies and Prevention, eds., C. Reyes, W.J. Rudman, and C.R. Hewitt, New York: Haworth Medical Press, 2002: 41–54; Klein, A., T. Tobin, A. Salomon, and J. Dubois, "A Statewide Profile of Abuse of Older Women and the Criminal Justice Response," Final report to the National Institute of Justice, grant number 2006-WB-BX-0009, April 2008, NCJ 222459, available at https://www.ncjrs.gov/pdffiles1/nij/grants/222459.pdf; Brandl, B., and J.A. Raymond, "Policy Implications of Recognizing that Caregiver Stress Is Not the Primary Cause of Elder Abuse," Generations, 36 (3) (2012): 32–39.

[26]Jackman, M.R., "Violence in Social Life," Annual Review of Sociology, 28 (2002): 387–415.

[27]Ansello, E.F., "Causes and Theories," in Abuse, Neglect and Exploitation of Older Persons: Strategies for Assessment and Intervention, eds., L.A.

Baumhover and S.C. Beall, Baltimore, Md.: Health Professions Press, 1996: 9–29; Laumann, Leitsch, and Waite, 2008; Wilber, K. H., and D.P. McNeilly, "Elder Abuse and Victimization," in Handbook of the Psychology of Aging, 5th ed., eds., J.E. Birren and K.W. Schaie, San Diego, Calif.: Academic Press, 2001: 569–591.

[28]Burnight, K., and L. Mosqueda, "Theoretical Model Development in Elder Mistreatment," Final report submitted to the National Institute of Justice, grant number 2005-IJ-CX-0048, May 2011, NCJ 234488, available at https://www.ncjrs.gov/pdffiles1/nij/grants/234488.pdf.

[29]Belsky, J., "Etiology of Child Maltreatment: A Developmental Ecological Analysis," Psychological Bulletin, 114 (3) (1993): 413–434; Kempe et al., 1962.

[30]Nerenberg, 2002; Steinmetz, 1978; Steinmetz, S.K., "Elder Abuse Is Caused by the Perception of Stress Associated with Providing Care," in Current Controversies on Family Violence, eds., D.R. Loseke, R.J. Gelles, and M.M. Cavanaugh, Thousand Oaks, Calif.: Sage, 2005: 191–206; Wolf, R.S., "The Nature and Scope of Elder Abuse," Generations, 24 (2000): 6–11.

[31]Bandura, A., Aggression: A Social Learning Analysis, Oxford, England: Prentice-Hall, 1973; Bandura, A., "Social Learning Theory of Aggression," Journal of Communication, 28 (3) (1978): 12–29.

[32]Ansello, 1996; Wilber and McNeilly, 2001.

[33]Homans, G.C., The Human Group, New York: Harcourt Brace; Homans, G.C. (1966). Social Behaviour: Its Elementary Forms, New York: Harcourt Brace, 1950.

[34]Decalmer, P., and F. Glendenning, The Mistreatment of Elderly People, London: Sage, 1993; see also Walker, A.J., and K.R. Allen, "Relationships Between Caregiving Daughters and Their Elderly Mothers," Gerontologist, 31 (3) (1991): 389–396.

[35]Riggs, D.S., and K.D. O'Leary, "A Theoretical Model of Courtship Aggression," in Violence in Dating Relationships: Emerging Social Issues, eds., M.A. Pirog-Good and J.E. Stets, New York: Praeger, 1989.

[36]Riggs, D.S., and K.D. O'Leary, "Aggression Between Heterosexual Dating Partners: An Examination of a Causal Model of Courtship Aggression," Journal of Interpersonal Violence, 11 (1996): 519–540.

[37]Yllo, K.A., and M. Bogard, eds., Feminist Perspectives on Wife Abuse, Newbury Park, Calif.: Sage, 1998.

[38]Yllo, K.A., "Through a Feminist Lens," in Current Controversies on Family Violence, eds., D.L. Loseke, R.J. Gelles, and M.M. Cavanaugh, Thousand Oaks, Calif.: Sage, 2005: 19–34.

[39]Brandl, B., "Power and Control: Understanding Domestic Abuse in Later Life, Generations, 24 (2) (2002): 39–45.

[40]Bronfenbrenner, U., The Ecology of Human Development: Experiments by Nature and Design, Boston: Harvard University Press, 1979.

[41]Dutton, D.G., "An Ecologically Nested Theory of Male Violence Toward Intimates," International Journal of Women's Studies, 8 (4) (1985): 404–413; Jasinski, J.L., "Theoretical Explanations for Violence Against Women," in Sourcebook on Violence Against Women, eds. C.M. Renzetti, J.L. Edleson, and R.K. Bergen, Thousand Oaks, Calif: Sage, 2001: 5–21.

[42]Schiamberg, L.B., and D. Gans, "An Ecological Framework for Contextual Risk Factors in Elder Abuse by Adult Children," Journal of Elder Abuse & Neglect, 11 (1) (1999): 79–105; Schiamberg, L.B., and D. Gans, "Elder Abuse by Adult Children: An Applied Ecological Framework for Understanding Contextual Risk Factors and the Intergenerational Character of Quality of Life," International Journal of Aging and Human Development, 50 (2000): 329–359.

[43]Engel, G.L., "The Need for a New Medical Model: A Challenge for Biomedicine, Science, 196 (4286) (1977): 129–136, doi:10.1126/science.847460.

[44]Ibid.

[45]Bonnie and Wallace, 2003.

[46]Ibid., 63; Maccoby, E.E., "The Uniqueness of Parent-Child Relationships," in Relationships as Developmental Contexts: The Minnesota Symposia on Child Psychology, eds., W.A. Collins and B. Laursen, Mahwah, N.J.: Lawrence Erlbaum Associates, 2000: 157–175.

[47]See Ansello, 1996; Burnight and Mosqueda, 2011; Laumann, Leitsch, and Waite, 2008; Wilber and McNeilly, 2001.

[48]Jackson, S.L., and T.L. Hafemeister, "Formulating Theory-Based Explanations for Four Distinct Types of Elder Maltreatment," under review, n.d.; See also Ansello, 1996.

[49]Clancy, M., B. McDaid, D. O'Neill, and J.G. O'Brien, "National Profiling of Elder Abuse Referrals," Age and Ageing, 40 (3) (2011): 346–352, doi:10.1093/ageing/afr023; Laumann, Leitsch, and Waite, 2008; National Center on Elder Abuse, The National Elder Abuse Incidence Study: Final Report, Washington, D.C.: American Public Human Services Association, 1998; Teaster, et al., 2006.

[50]Cook, J.A., "Who 'Mothers' the Chronically Mentally Ill?," Family Relations, 37 (1) (1988), 42–49; Greenberg, J.S., M. Mailick Seltzer, and J.R. Greenley, "Aging Parents of Adults with Disabilities: The Gratification and Frustrations of Later-Life Caregiving," The Gerontologist, 33 (4) (1993): 542–550; Jackson and Hafemeister, under review, n.d.; Anetzberger, G., The Etiology of Elder Abuse by Adult Offspring, Springfield, Ill.: Charles C. Thomas, 1987.

[51]Finch, J., Family Obligations and Social Change, Cambridge, Mass.: Polity Press, 1989.

[52]Wright, J.L., "Guardianship for Your Own Good: Improving the Well-Being of Respondents and Wards in the USA," International Journal of Law and Psychiatry, 33 (5–6) (2010): 350–368.

[53]Hafemeister, T.L., and M. Weger, "Necessary Fiduciaries: Protecting Our Elderly from Financial Exploitation," manuscript in preparation, 2012.

[54]Jackson and Hafemeister, 2011; MetLife Mature Market Institute, "Broken Trust: Elders, Family and Finance," Study conducted by the MetLife Mature Market Institute, the National Committee for the Prevention of Elder Abuse, and the Center for Gerontology at Virginia Polytechnic Institute and State University, March 2009, accessed February 2010 at http://www.metlife.com/assets/cao/mmi/publications/studies/mmi-study-broken-trust-elders-family-finances.pdf.

[55]Pittaway, E.D., A. Westhues, and T. Peressini, "Risk Factors for Abuse and Neglect Among Older Adults," The Gerontologist, 43 (S1) (1995): 19–28.

[56]Jackson and Hafemeister, 2011.

[57]Braithwaite, J., "White Collar Crime," Annual Review of Sociology, 11

(1985): 1–25; Coleman, J.W., "Toward an Integrated Theory of White-Collar Crime," American Journal of Sociology, 93 (1987): 406–439; Piquero, N.L., and M.L. Benson, "White-Collar Crime and Criminal Careers: Specifying a Trajectory of Punctuated Situational Offending," Journal of Contemporary Criminal Justice, 20 (2) (2004): 148–165, doi:10.1177/1043986204263770.

[58]Burnight and Mosqueda, 2011.

[59]Jackson and Hafemeister, under review, n.d.; Jackson and Hafemeister, 2011.

[60]Biggs, S., and I. Haapala, "Theoretical Development and Elder Mistreatment: Spreading Awareness and Conceptual Complexity in Examining the Management of Socio-Emotional Boundaries," Ageing International, 35 (2010): 171–184; McGuire, J., Understanding Psychology and Crime: Perspectives on Theory and Action, Berkshire, U.K.: Open University Press, 2004; Pillemer, 2005.

[61]Band-Winterstein, T., and Z. Eisikovits, "Towards a Phenomenological Theorizing About Old Women Abuse," Ageing International, 35 (2010): 202–214.

[62]Bengtson, V.L., D. Gans, N.M. Putney, and M. Silversmith, Handbook of Theories of Aging, 2nd ed., New York: Springer, 2009; Hooyman, N.R., and H.A. Kiyak, Social Gerontology: A Multidisciplinary Perspective, Boston: Allyn & Bacon, 1988.

[63]Anderson, J.F., and L. Dyson, Criminological Theories: Understanding Crime in America, Lanham, Md.: University Press of America, 2002; Cohen, L.E., and M. Felson, "Social Change and Crime Rate Trends: A Routine Activity Approach," American Sociological Review, 44 (1979): 588–608; Payne, B.K., Crime and Elder Abuse: An Integrated Perspective, 2nd ed., Springfield, Ill.: Charles C. Thomas, 2005; Setterlund, D., C. Tilse, J. Wilson, A. McCawley, and L. Rosenman, "Understanding Financial Elder Abuse in Families: The Potential of Routine Activities Theory," Ageing & Society, 27 (2007): 599–614.

[64]Ansello, 1996; Wilber and McNeilly, 2001; Wolf, R.S., "Elder Abuse and Neglect: Causes and Consequences," Journal of Geriatric Psychiatry, 30 (1997): 153–174.

[65]Penhale, B., "Older Women, Domestic Violence, and Elder Abuse: A Review of Commonalities, Differences, and Shared Approaches," Journal of Elder

Abuse and Neglect, 15 (3) (2003): 163–183.

[66]Schiamberg and Gans, 1999; Schiamberg and Gans, 2000.

[67]Jackson and Hafemeister, under review, n.d.

[68]Kinnear, P., and A. Graycar, "Abuse of Older People: Crime or Family Dynamics?," Trends and Issues in Crime and Criminal Justice, 113 (May 1999): 1–6.

[69]Gordon, R.M., and D. Brill, "The Abuse and Neglect of the Elderly," International Journal of Law & Psychiatry, 24 (2001): 183–197; Penhale, 2003, 171; Phillips, L.R., "Elder Abuse: What Is It? Who Says So?," Geriatric Nursing, 4 (1983): 167–170.

[70]Bonnie and Wallace, 2003, 65.

[71]Jackson and Hafemeister, 2011.

[72]Jackman, 2002.

[73]Doerner, W.G., and S.P. Lab, Victimology. Newark, N.J.: Lexis Nexis Matthew Bender, 2008; Wallace, H., Victimology: Legal, Psychological, and Social Perspectives, Boston: Pearson/Allyn & Bacon, 2007.

[74]Jackson, S.L., and T.L. Hafemeister, "Assessing the Interpersonal Dynamics Associated with Four Types of Elder Maltreatment," manuscript in preparation, n.d.

[75]Ibid.

[76]Payne, B.K., "An Integrated Understanding of Elder Abuse and Neglect," Journal of Criminal Justice, 30 (2002): 535–547.

[77]Jackson, S.L., and T.L. Hafemeister, "Final Report: Financial Abuse of the Elderly vs. Other Forms of Elder Abuse: Assessing Their Dynamics, Risk Factors, and Society's Response," Final report to the National Institute of Justice, grant number 2006-WG-BX-0010, August 2010, NCJ 233613, available at https://www.ncjrs.gov/pdffiles1/nij/grants/233613.pdf.

[78]Jackson and Hafemeister, 2010.

[79]Jackson and Hafemeister, 2011.

[80]Jackson, S.L., and T.L. Hafemeister, "How Case Characteristics Differ Across Four Types of Elder Maltreatment: Implications for Tailoring Interventions to Increase Victim Safety," Journal of Applied Gerontology, published online before print (September 2012), doi:10.1177/0733464812459370.

[81]Jackson and Hafemeister, manuscript in preparation, n.d.

[82]Jackson, S.L., and T.L. Hafemeister, "Enhancing the Safety of Elderly Victims After the Close of an APS Investigation," Journal of Interpersonal Violence, 28 (6) (April 2013): 1223-1239, doi:10.1177/0886260512468241.

[83]Jackson and Hafemeister, under review, n.d.

[84]Ibid.

[85]See Jackson and Hafemeister, under review, n.d., for a full description of these theories.

[86]See Jackson, S.L., and T.L. Hafemeister, "Elder Financial Exploitation vs. Hybrid Financial Exploitation Co-occurring with Physical Abuse and/or Neglect," Psychology of Violence, 2 (3) (July 2012): 285–296, doi:10.1037/a0027273.

[87]Brownell, P., and D. Heiser, "Psycho-Educational Support Groups for Older Women Victims of Family Mistreatment: A Pilot Study," in Elder Abuse and Mistreatment: Policy, Practice, and Research, eds., M.J. Mellor and P. Brownell, New York: The Haworth Press, 2006: 145–160; Jackson and Hafemeister, 2011; Neale, A.V., M. Hwalek, C.S. Goodrich, and K.M. Quinn, "Reasons for Case Closure Among Substantiated Reports of Elder Abuse," The Journal of Applied Gerontology, 16 (4) (1997): 442–458; Pillemer, K., "The Dangers of Dependency: New Findings on Domestic Violence Against the Elderly," Social Problems, 33 (1985): 146–158; Vinton, L., "Factors Associated with Refusing Services Among Maltreated Elderly," Journal of Elder Abuse & Neglect, 3 (2) (1991): 89–103.

[88]Jackson and Hafemeister, 2011.

[89]Ibid.; Jackson and Hafemeister, July 2012; Jackson and Hafemeister, 2013.

[90]Burnight and Mosqueda, 2011.

[91]Ibid.

[92]Quinn and Zielke, 2005.

[93]Brownell, P., J. Berman, and A. Salamone, "Mental Health and Criminal Justice Issues Among Perpetrators of Elder Abuse," Journal of Elder Abuse and Neglect, 11 (4) (1999): 81–94; Pillemer, 2005.

[94]Jackson and Hafemeister, 2011.

[95]Bonnie and Wallace, 2003.

[96]Kuhn, T., The Structure of Scientific Revolutions, Chicago: University of Chicago Press, 1962.

[97]Quinn and Zielke, 2005; Benson, 2008.

[98]Pillemer, 2005.

[99]Dixon, J., J. Manthorpe, S. Biggs, A. Mowlam, R. Temmant, A. Tinker, and C. McCreadie, "Defining Elder Mistreatment: Reflections on the United Kingdom Study of Abuse and Neglect of Older People," Ageing & Society, 30 (2010): 403–420. doi:10.1017/S0144686X0999047X.

[100]Jackson and Hafemeister, 2011; MetLife Mature Market Institute, 2009.

[101]Jackson and Hafemeister, manuscript in preparation, n.d.

[102]He, W., M. Sengupta, V. Velkoff, and K.A. DeBarros, 65+ in the United States: Current Population Reports, Special Studies. Washington, D.C.: U.S. Census Bureau, 2005.

[103]Johnson, K.D., Financial Crimes Against the Elderly, Problem-Oriented Guides for Police, Problem-Specific Guides Series, no. 20. Washington, D.C.: U.S. Department of Justice, Office of Community Oriented Policing Services, 2003; Lewis, T., "Fifty Ways to Exploit Your Grandmother: The Status of Financial Abuse of the Elderly in Minnesota," William Mitchell Law Review, 28 (2001): 911–954.

[104]Jackson and Hafemeister, manuscript in preparation, n.d.

[105]National Adult Protective Services Association (NAPSA) and the National Committee for the Prevention of Elder Abuse (NCPEA), Guiding Principles for Research in Adult Protective Services, Springfield, Ill.: NAPSA and Washington, D.C.: NCPEA, n.d., available at http://www.napsa-now.org/wp-content/uploads/2012/06/Guiding-Principles1.pdf; NAPSA and NCPEA,

Guidelines for Evaluating and Applying Research in Adult Protective Services, Springfield, Ill.: NAPSA and Washington, D.C.: NCPEA, n.d., available at http://www.preventelderabuse.org/about/documents/NAPSA_NCPEA_GUIDELINES_FOR_EVALUATING_AND_APPLYING_RESEARCH.FINAL.pdf.

[106]Lachs and Berman, 2011.

[107]Bonnie and Wallace, 2003.

[108]Johnson, M. P., "Patriarchal Terrorism and Common Couple Violence: Two Forms of Violence Against Women," Journal of Marriage and Family, 57 (2) (1995): 283–294.

[109]See, for example, Nerenberg, 2002.

[110]Blenkner, M., M. Bloom, and M. Nielson, "A Research and Demonstration Project of Protective Services," Social Casework, 52 (1971): 483–499.

[111]Ploeg, J., J. Fear, B. Hutchison, H. MacMillan, and G. Bolan, "A Systematic Review of Interventions for Elder Abuse," Journal of Elder Abuse & Neglect, 21 (2009): 187–210.

[112]Daniel, B., and A. Bowes, "Re-Thinking Harm and Abuse: Insights From a Lifespan Perspective," British Journal of Social Work, 41 (2011): 820–836.

[113]He, Sengupta, Velkoff, and DeBarros, 2005.

[114]Rossi, P.H., M.W. Lipsey, and H.E. Freeman, Evaluation: A Systematic Approach, 7th ed., Thousand Oaks, Calif.: Sage, 2004.

[115]Hwalek, M.A., A.V. Neale, C.S. Goodrich, and K. Quinn, "The Association of Elder Abuse and Substance Abuse in the Illinois Elder Abuse System," The Gerontologist, 36 (5) (1996): 694–700, doi:10.1093/geront/36.5.694; Jackson and Hafemeister, 2011; Jackson and Hafemeister, July 2012; Libes Simon, M., An Exploratory Study of Adult Protective Services Programs' Repeat Elder Abuse Clients, Washington, D.C.: American Association of Retired Persons, 1992; McCreadie, C., "A Review of Research Outcomes in Elder Abuse," The Journal of Adult Protection, 4 (2002): 3–8; Nordstrom, N., "Perpetrators of Abuse and Neglect," in Abuse and Neglect of Vulnerable Adult Populations, ed. J.M. Otto, Kingston, N.J.: Civic Research Institute, 2005.

**About the authors:**

**Shelly L. Jackson** is an Assistant Professor of Psychiatry and Neurobehavioral Sciences at the Institute of Law, Psychiatry and Public Policy, University of Virginia.

**Thomas L. Hafemeister** is an Associate Professor at the University of Virginia School of Law, University of Virginia, and an Associate Professor of Medical Education, Department of Psychiatry and Neurobehavioral Sciences, School of Medicine, University of Virginia.

Supported under award no. 2006-WG-BX-0010 from the National Institute of Justice, U.S. Department of Justice. Points of view in this paper are those of the authors and do not necessarily represent the official position of the U.S. Department of Justice or the University of Virginia.

The National Institute of Justice is the research, development and evaluation agency of the U.S. Department of Justice.  NIJ's mission is to advance scientific research, development and evaluation to enhance the administration of justice and public safety.

The National Institute of Justice is a component of the Office of Justice Programs, which also includes the Bureau of Justice Assistance; the Bureau of Justice Statistics; the Community Capacity Development Office; the Office for Victims of Crime; the Office of Juvenile Justice and Delinquency Prevention; and the Office of Sex Offender Sentencing, Monitoring, Apprehending, Registering, and Tracking (SMART).

www.ingramcontent.com/pod-product-compliance
Lightning Source LLC
Chambersburg PA
CBHW070519290526
45790CB00003B/1257